HOW CAN I HELP?

Questions & Answers About Manners

By Barbara Shook Hazen
Illustrated by Lynn Sweat

Cover by Stuart Trotter

GALLERY BOOKS
An Imprint of W. H. Smith Publishers Inc.
112 Madison Avenue
New York City 10016

Why are "please" and "thank you" called magic words?

Because they work like magic to make people want to do things for you. Someone is much more likely to get you a glass of juice, for example, if you say, "May I please have some juice?" and "Thank you" when you receive it. Using "please" and "thank you" shows good manners.

What are good manners?

They are the way you act toward other people. They make whatever you do more pleasant. Good manners show that you appreciate what others do for you.

Let me help with those packages.

Would you like to use my crayons?

Are there any other magic words?

"Excuse me" are magic words because they can be used in many different situations. If you cough, sneeze, hiccup or yawn, it's polite to cover your mouth and say "excuse me." "Excuse me" also comes in handy when you want to leave the table or have to interrupt someone who is talking.

Why isn't it polite to make fun of other people?

Because you will hurt their feelings. If someone trips or falls down, for example, don't laugh or point. Help them up, and ask if they're all right.

Should I be polite even when someone isn't polite to me?

You should always be polite. If you use good manners, other people are more likely to use them, too.

How do I use good manners at home?

Your family is very special. They like to be appreciated and treated with consideration. This means helping around the house, keeping your room neat, and being kind and thoughtful.

How should I behave with a babysitter?

You should be polite and helpful. Say "please" and "thank you" when asking for something. Suggest games or activities you could do together. Help the sitter find something if she or he doesn't know where it is.

The glasses are in this cabinet, Joan.

What are good phone manners?

When you answer the phone, say "Hello, this is John James," or "Hello, James' residence." Then get the person being called or take a message if that person can't come to the phone. Remember to give the message to the person as soon as possible. When someone else is on the phone be quiet so that the person can hear what is being said. Don't interrupt, unless it's an emergency.

PHONE MESSAGES

FOR _Mom_

CALLER _Mrs. Jones_

TIME _____

TEL. NO. _____

MESSAGE _____

_____

How should I answer the doorbell?

First, ask the grown-up in charge *if* you should answer it. Greet someone you know with their name and a friendly welcome like, "Hi, Mrs. James. Please come in. I'll let Mom know you're here." If it's someone you don't know, tell the person to wait while you get a grown-up.

Are there special manners for when we eat?

Yes. Good table manners include coming to the table on time, putting your napkin in your lap, eating slowly and quietly, and using "please" and "thank you."

Why are good table manners important?

They make mealtimes pleasant for everyone. Eating is more fun when you take the time to enjoy the food and the people you're eating with.

What if I'm eating in a restaurant?

Use your very best table manners. Talk quietly, be patient even if things seem to take a long time, and don't get upset if something doesn't taste the way you expected. Trying new food is part of the adventure of eating out.

What do I do with my napkin?

When you sit down, unfold your napkin and put it in your lap. If you leave the table during the meal, put your napkin on the chair. At the end of the meal, leave it on the table to the left of the plate.

Oops! I knocked over a glass of water. Now, what do I do?

Accidents happen to everybody, even grown-ups. Say you're sorry and clean up as best you can. Then forget about it and enjoy the rest of the meal.

What should I do when there's something new and yukky-looking on my plate?

Try at least one bite. You just might like it. If you don't, leave the rest on your plate. You don't need to go into a long explanation.

How do I ask for something I want?

Ask with a "please," and accept with a "thank you." If your mouth is full, wait until you finish chewing before you speak.

Which piece should I take when something is offered to me?

Make sure which one you want before you touch anything. Then take the one you touch. If everything on the plate is the same, take the one nearest to you.

How do I pass food to someone?

Pass food around, not across, the table. Pass a platter with both hands. Pass a pitcher or a knife with its handle toward the person reaching for it.

There are so many forks and spoons at the table. Which one do I use?

Use the spoon on the outside first. Soup comes before ice cream, so use the large spoon on the outside first. Salad usually comes before the main course so use the small salad fork on the outside first.

How do I set the table?

The napkin and forks are on the left side of the plate. The knife and spoons are on the right. The glass is also on the right above the plate and the salad plate is on the left. This jingle might help you. "Spoons and knife on the right. The rest is on the left." Remember that being helpful is more important than having everything exactly right.

What foods can I eat with my fingers?

Things that aren't messy and don't come off on your fingers, like cookies, carrot sticks, grapes and most sandwiches. If you're not sure about something, like fried chicken, watch the grown-ups at the table, or ask.

What should I do when I'm invited to a friend's house?

Ask your parents if you can go. Reply by calling or by sending a note as soon as possible. Be sure you know the date and the time you are to go.

Is there a special way to behave at a friend's house?

Obey the rules of the house, be careful when using your friend's toys, and thank your friend and the grown-up in charge when you leave.

How do I introduce a friend to a grown-up?

It's polite to say the name of the grown-up first. For example, "Mom, this is Jamie, my friend from school," or "Mr. Smith, this is my friend Ann."

Mrs. Brown, this is my friend Mark.

What about introducing one friend to another friend?

Say both names and something about the person you're introducing. For example, "Marcie, this is Ted. He used to live next door."
"Ted, this is Marcie. She's a friend from school."

Should I ever introduce myself?

Yes, when you are at a party or somewhere where there are people you don't know. It is particularly thoughtful to introduce yourself to someone who seems shy or who doesn't know anyone. Say something like, "Hi, I'm Amy. We live in the green house on the corner. What's your name?"

When should I shake hands?

When you are saying "hello" or "goodbye," or being introduced to someone who offers you his or her hand. Extend your right hand and grasp the person's hand firmly.

What is the polite way to talk to someone?

When you talk, look at the person you are talking to and speak clearly. When the other person is talking, listen carefully. Wait until the other person has finished before you speak again.

Excuse me, Mary, your mother wants you home right away.

What if I have something important to say while other people are talking?

If you have to interrupt someone who is speaking, say "excuse me."

What is the best way to make friends?

The best way to make a friend is to be a friend. Be fun, caring, and loyal. Share your toys and your feelings. Treat your friend the way you'd like to be treated.

What if my friend and I have a fight?

Being friends doesn't mean always agreeing with each other. Part of the fun of friendship is being with someone whose thoughts and feelings aren't exactly the same as yours. The important thing is to be able to disagree without fighting. If you do fight, say you're sorry afterwards and be friends again.

My teacher says I should be a good sport. What *is* a good sport?

A good sport is someone who plays fairly, thinks of the team first, and plays for the fun of it—not just to win. Good sports get more fun out of any game.

Why is it nice to share?

Sharing is generous and polite. If you have something you don't want to share, put it away before your friend comes over. You can play with it later. Remember that the more you share, the more others will share with you.

When friends come to visit should I let them go first?

If you have a guest, it's good manners to let your guest have the first turn on the slide, the first choice of a game, or the first cookie.

What if my friend wants to do something I don't?

As the host you should go along with what your guest wants to do. After awhile, however, you could suggest something else you both might like to do.

Are there special manners for places like the library?

Yes. The library is another place to use your best manners. Speak quietly so you don't disturb people who are reading. Treat books like friends. Turn the pages carefully, and return the books to their places when you're finished.

What about a museum?

A museum is a little like a library when it comes to manners. Speak softly, walk slowly, and don't lean on the display cases or touch anything you're not supposed to. Behave so that you'll be welcomed back, and so that your parents will want to bring you again.

What if someone's in my way, or I can't see?

Say, "excuse me, please," or wait until the person moves and you can get a better view.

Are there any other places where good manners are important?

Yes, when you're traveling. If you're taking a bus, quietly find an empty seat and sit down. Keep your feet tucked in, speak in a low voice, and apologize if you accidentally step on someone's toes. Offer your seat to an older person, or to someone with a baby or an armload of packages.

What if I'm traveling in the car?

Safety and good manners go together in a car. Stay in your seat, wear your seat belt and speak quietly. If it's going to be a long trip bring a book or a game with you. Be considerate of the driver and the other passengers.

There seem to be so many manners to remember. How will I know if I'm doing the right thing?

The most important thing to remember is to treat other people the same way you would like to be treated.